The story's

Writing to support
wildlife at risk

26

Supporting The Wildlife Trusts

First published in 2020
by 26 Characters Ltd
32 Parker Street
London WC2B 5PH

ISBN 978-1-9162665-1-3

British Library Cataloguing in Publication Data.
A catalogue record for this book is available from
the British Library.

Designed by David Carroll & Co
Edited by Sue Evans and Lisa Andrews
Cover image by Therese Kieran
26 Wild logo by Mark Noad
Typeface Zenon by Riccardo Olocco
Printed by Hickling & Squires
Printed on Nautilus Classic White (100% recycled)

Published in partnership with the Royal Society of
Wildlife Trusts, The Kiln, Waterside, Mather Road,
Newark, Nottinghamshire NG24 1WT.

We are honoured to have collaborated with The Wildlife Trusts for this project on vulnerable species. It seems meant-to-be after last year's project on trees with Woodland Trust. This book, *The story's not over*, is a companion anthology to sit alongside *The Understory*.

There's a close connection between the disappearance of wild species and the loss of habitat. Recovery is needed in all kinds of habitats to make sure we don't lose these animals whose roles are vital in nature's cycle. The Wildlife Trusts provided 26 with the list of 52 vulnerable UK species, and we randomly paired these animals with writers. Four writers took a global view to write about species threatened in other parts of the world.

As writers we approach these amazing animals as stories to be told: stories help to connect emotively with readers. The writers have become champions for each species; voices for natural recovery.

We do that in a form invented by 26 – the centena, 100 words exactly, with the first three words repeated as the final three. With this we intend to say that extinction is not the inevitable end. The story goes on. There is still time for recovery, if we are determined.

John Simmons, co-founder 26

Our natural world is in trouble. Wildlife is disappearing at an alarming rate and the threat of climate catastrophe is ever present. We live in a time of emergency and the future can feel bleak.

But we know that it does not need to be like this. There is hope, and people are the answer. If we act now, we can turn things around and look forward to a wilder future, where nature thrives and people become better connected into the natural world, benefitting our health, wellbeing and prosperity.

That's why we were delighted to be approached by 26 to collaborate on a project that has created a set of wonderful, evocative and stirring stories of wildlife under threat in the United Kingdom and further afield. By telling the story of some of our beloved – and less loved or well known, but equally important – wildlife, we hope that more people will take note and join our mission for nature's recovery, taking action for the wildlife that has given us so much. The writers' accounts of 'their' creatures cannot fail to inspire – I hope that you enjoy these impassioned centenas, take heart that you are part of the solution for a wilder future and get active!

Joanna Richards, The Wildlife Trusts

These species are disappearing.

BEAVER
LADYBIRD SPIDER
SHORT-SNOUTED SEAHORSE
RED SQUIRREL
PIPISTRELLE BAT
ROSEATE TERN
UNDULATE RAY
HEDGEHOG
PUFFIN
GRIZZLED SKIPPER BUTTERFLY
WHITE-CLAWED CRAYFISH
SKYLARK
BROWN HARE
EUROPEAN EEL
HEATH TIGER BEETLE
BLUE SHARK
SAND LIZARD
SMALL HEATH BUTTERFLY
CORN BUNTING
COMMON SKATE
CUCKOO
NARROW-HEADED ANT
PEARL-BORDERED FRITILLARY BUTTERFLY
COD
HARBOUR PORPOISE
LESSER SPOTTED WOODPECKER
KOALA
EUROPEAN WILD HAMSTER

Can we help them recover?

ARCHEY'S FROG
PANGOLIN
NATIVE OYSTERS
HEATH FRITILLARY BUTTERFLY
SHRILL CARDER BEE
WILLOW TIT
NOBLE CHAFER
SMOOTH SNAKE
FEN RAFT SPIDER
GREY LONG-EARED BAT
COMMON TOAD
TURTLE DOVE
KITTIWAKE
GARDEN TIGER MOTH
MOUNTAIN HARE
WHITE-FACED DARTER
BILBERRY BUMBLEBEE
GLOW-WORM
LATTICED HEATH MOTH
HAZEL DORMOUSE
PINE MARTEN
WILDCAT
WATER VOLE
SPOTTED FLYCATCHER
WALL BROWN BUTTERFLY
NATTERJACK TOAD
STAG BEETLE
NIGHTINGALE

The sight of a beaver

Ripples spill out across the pond
and [   ] cruises into view
suspicion in her eye—
            as if dispatching peaceful creatures was
            still a sport for hat-makers
—she dips beneath the surface

Motes twist in ribbons of shadow
and the quiet puts another mile between here
    and the A30
McDonald's and 18-wheelers

From her kingdom,
water lapping at the jamb,
the web-foot engineer
invites us to save tomorrow
gnaws, digs, builds
better to show than tell—
            the master knows
—that even at the brink of excess
from the actions of one dedicated soul
generations can flourish
the way ripples spill out

A most elusive velvet spider

Lost, presumed extinct.

Over seven decades unseen.

Unrecorded.

Underground, midnight black [   ] kept spinning.
Secreted in sandy, silk-lined burrows,
Capped with entrapping canopies.

Emerging, only to leave home in gorse-scented
    springtime
as spiderlings or,
As mature males, strutting out amongst the
    stones and heather;
Resplendent in scarlet totty-hunting jackets with
    six black velvet buttons.

[   ]'s lowland heath habitat fragmented.

 Lost.

To: Fields – ploughed.
     Forests – planted.
     Concrete – poured.

Then, BINGO!
[   ] was spotted,
Reclaiming its dot on the map.

Forty years later, [   ] remains vulnerable.
Rare.
Sustained by a visionary web of care.

No longer lost, presumed extinct.

Short-snouted seahorse

So little space
for the sweet whisper
of salt water through seagrass,
dawn filter of sunlight
through leaves, seeds, plankton.

But part this sway, this green
underwater meadow
(dancefloor, nursery, larder),
here's an enigma:

[   ]

Cryptic colour-changers,
they dance together
at dawn in white
and stand all day proud
as gentlemen in dappled Sunday
waistcoats, chest out, elbows in,
shadow fluttering
in the shallows, our hidden

ancestors, strange fish,
unknowable codes: they see you
in full colour. Monthly he births
their young, holds tight
as we uproot their home,
keeps clinging, keeps dancing
though we've left them
so
little
space.

Red Squirrels, Iain's garden

Through the hedge they come, only two this time,
    skirting the garden shed.
Iain, the artist, bends, tending his plants; bright
    splashes of colour he envisaged in
dreary winter when his rare russet visitors nestled
    quiet in trees.
On their foray today they pay him no heed,
Nor, it seems, he them, though he welcomes their
    passage.
"Nutkins," he mutters.
Regardless, they flow, copper-coloured in sunlight,
    through this patch of paradise,
over the high back fence, seeking treasure in Spruce
    trees, hung wealthy with cones.
Evening darkens. Iain, cosy indoors, watches,
    wistful,
As shadow tails disappear back through the hedge.

In flight as night falls

It's so small.
Thumb-sized,
light as a coin in your palm.

After sunset, [   ] leaves its eaves,
darting through dusky sky,
seeking moths, midges, mosquitoes.
It flits along woodland rivers, high above urban
    gardens.
Its nightly in-flight dining taking thousands
    of bugs.

Bony black wings, a mask of dark fur.
A bad press maybe.
But this is no villain.
A pollinator, a pest controller –
its numbers drop amid chemical crops.
Renovated rafters raise a toxic threat.

A little welcome might just save this tiny creature,
a box house here, a friendly garden there.
It's an easy gesture.

It's so small.

The roseate tern

Disappearing from view, the [   ] descends
Plunging
it dives
down
into the deep
for fish
to feed the hungry next in line

The timid [   ] finds
sanctuary
on remote rocks
crumbling into the sea
sheltering
from relentless rain
and unforgiving winds
here is safer
nesting, away
from the call of the gulls
and hands
plucking them
from the skies

Black caps
Trapped, starved, displaced
Become threatened and rare
And flashes of pink turn red

But the tide is turning

Almost ghost-like
the [   ] takes flight
tail feathers streaming against the blue
it climbs
high
Soaring upwards, before disappearing from view

Almost erased

To witness them
you might need
to dive a lifetime
glimpsing one,
maybe two,
of these pancake-thin beauties
skating the ocean floor,
dipping and furling
like a chiffon hem,
pencilled with
undulating lines and flecks
as unique as any human face
until seized
in the bycatch of commercial fisheries
and almost erased.

Yet individuals are traced
to the same site
on the same day
years apart,
guided by an internal GPS
whose wavelength we do not understand.
When recognised
exhilaration surges,
the instinct to protect
arises,
the knowledge that we can
is known,
should we choose to witness them.

But

When I'm gone
my little ones will be big ones
wanting to be like me.
But perhaps not.

Here I am [   ]
in the garden trying to go
into the next garden.
But cannot.

And I want to wander
snuffling into the woods
across the road.
But dare not.

Let's understand each other.

I like to climb trees
and swim in water.
I really do.

I need hedgerows
and wild pastures.
But they have gone.

Your cars kill me,
your builders block my way,
your farmers poison my food.

But you'll probably say
you miss me,
when I'm gone.

Puffin's Soliloquy

The clifftop clown, us [   ] learn a craft
Of comic landings, wet fish, clumsy walks,
Painted and stockinged, a carnival raft—
Though wearing this beak can get rather *awks*!
Must I play the fool? Pray, hear my sorrow:
Warm tides, storm clouds and fleeting sand eels,
They've left me puffing – forecast a burrow's
Empty fate – wherever is my yearned-for mate?
Courage [   ]! The circus must go on—
And yet this gaudy mask ill-fits my mood,
Preening, loafing, dwindling, tending to brood
O love, can you be so late? Spare a laugh
Ruin'd nature, shed a tear for the clifftop clown.

Grizzled skipper butterfly

Show me how we begin
where you unfurl
dispatch me

into the blue woo-hoo, when
your black spangled robes
separate

do not hesitate
dark damsel
come light my heather, show me

where you begin, myriad
no more
under the small blue flowers

in the leaf shadowed place
lift up lift up
hairy fairy, those that take you for moths

they haven't seen you. Make me true
fey wanderer, when I pick up a stone
and it grows warm in my hand

when there
is nothing except what is wanted
and weary we turn to the sun

[   ] show me how.

Lament of the white-clawed crayfish

Camouflaged, not vanished
I scuttle to the riffle
Where the ripple rolls crisp downstream

To the long-ago dusk.
Claypots drop – plop – beneath Miller's Bridge and
Copper kettles whistle for the harvest moon.

Your fresh fingers free me
Into the tannin squelch of river mulch.

My crevice calls,
[   ]

The signal sounds,
[   ]

I lie low in leaf litter,
Brittle limbs scratching your Father's line and
Dancing ragged spirals in the wastewater.

A plague runs under Miller's Bridge.
This carapace forged of old iron
Ruins to rust.

Will you whistle my lament to the harvest moon?
I was camouflaged not vanished.

Skylark

Easing the blue Vauxhall Astra into the dusty
  field-side car park,
Strawberry rows criss-crossed by straw, poking
  my flip-flopped feet.
1988. 'A' levels sat, driving test passed, about to
  spread my wings.
Mum leads the way, a punnet on each arm; pick
  one, eat one, while
Song rains down from the brown speck high
  above us.
'[   ]' says Mum, shading her eyes, squinting up
  at contrails and cumulus.
It's a sound-chute, and I stand under it, showering
  my head,
Shaking loose those last clinging roots.
Curve of brackeny wood at field margin, and that
  zipper of song, easing the blue.

The hare

Deepen the dark sky and frame the skeleton moon.
The meadow below is silent.

Hidden within, a delicate pulse of life.
Burst of springtime. Blossom of fur.

Wide-eyed and watchful, as hands reach through
    the night
with bloody efficiency.

Hammering hearts shelter beneath the passing breeze.

Hush

The trespassers listen.

Wait

A step breaks the silence.

There

The grass shudders and parts.

Too late

The path ahead vanishes.

Nowhere to hide, that delicate pulse of life.
Springtime is torn open, and the blossom is scattered.

The meadow is silent again,
and the skeleton moon
watches

as we deepen the dark.

European eel

What am I?
I am an *Anguilla anguilla*.
Grown in mud and birthed from guts
I am stolen, smuggled, hunted
dissected, gulped and glugged.
I am the last supper, garnished with oranges.
I am the King of Fiji, disguised as Sina's pet.
Aristotle, Freud or Pliny the Elder
no greedy human can place my elvers.
I am born from drops of dew
Satin, slippery, smooth.
I am guided by the moon.
A translucent tributary en route.
I am a curiosity, an unsolved riddle.
I am the limits of human knowledge.
I am a torment, yet tormented too.
What am I?

Hunting tigers on the heath

Watch it go.
A lightning flash of grizzled limbs
across this narrow domain,
glassy eyes locked on elusive prey.
Scuttle, skit, halt, reset,
then on again, piercing jaws agape.

A far cry from measured youth
when it lurked alone,
cased in sand.
Propelled only by hunger
to snatch a juicy passer-by,
drag it down and suck it dry.

Unexpected on a mild Surrey heath,
such lunges and throes.
But half the [   ] are gone
in a single generation.
The homebody made homeless.
The little biter bit.

We goggle at such ferocity for life
and indignantly refuse to watch it go.

Take Blue Off the Menu

I paint blue,
  not caring if splatters pollock
my white shirt;
            caught up in the curves
              of a nylon brush,
its undulating swirls
                  swerving the edge
        to change course;
            wild pelagic peregrinations
        through
    turquoise, cobalt, ultramarine
    become a steady pectoral glide
          from page to page,
      until *waters run deep* into finning;
dorsals hacked off for morsels
          reportedly tasteless;
    blue butchered alive,
  bloodied, thrown back, shock
        filling bowl-shaped eyes,
full stops sliding off
    tubular blown out snouts,
  white undersides spinning down
        to deepest blue,
          to the upside
              downturned smiles
              underpainting
                in vermillion hues,
                smears, splashes
                  thrashing tradition
                    I paint blue.

The [Sand] Lizard King

I Am King,
       Lacerta – true lizard; Lord of Animals.

Sun King. The star worships me:
       submits its shafts to stoke my blood;
       burnish my robes this dignified emerald.

Jade Warrior. A gem that glints in the dunes.
       My tongue flicks to caress
       the grasshopper's scent. Insect sacrifice.

Sand Shaman. I discard my whiplash tail;
       summon another to sprout.
       I'm healer, diviner, sorcerer, creator.

Great Pharaoh. I dismiss the sun; shrink the days;
       venture to the underworld
       to slink into your dreams and fantasies.

Lord of Light and Shadow. Every autumn entombed;
       every spring my resurrection.
       Incandescent. Immortal.

I Am King.

The flutterings of a small heath butterfly

Life is short but full of light as I flutter low over the grassy landscape. Sunshine draws me across heathland and hedgerow. The odd roadside verge adds variety. From April onwards I witness nature's shift from spring to summer in the vegetation along my path. I travel largely incognito, a brief stutter of pale orange, the all-seeing eyes on my wings focused on the ground. Only small creatures furrowing below can appreciate their beauty. But as I land and fold my wings back those secret eyes come briefly into view. September comes too soon, heralding my end. Life is short.

Corn bunting

An everyday sound, a reassuring clink of presence,
a jangling challenge, this dowdy minstrel claims the
land for his own. Sturdy and sepia-tinted, dressed
in dark furrows, umber streaks on tan and wheat,
[   ] watches his mate tend eggs of baked earth and
shadow in a cup of grass.

Workaday gleaner, once common companion,
changing fortunes reflecting customs of farm and
field. Gone from most in the span of one lifetime.

The receding tide of its presence carefully recorded,
fading into history in the lands of legend, keys
stilled, leaving an echo of what once was an
everyday sound.

Common skate on a porcelain plate

On porcelain plates with parsley butter amongst
the clang of Belfast's fish bars is where you might
see him. He looks a bit like a 'Ray', but that's his less
elusive cousin. Perfect with a crisp white.

White Atlantic skies slice the horizon in half over the
Celtic Sea. The largest of his kind, but it's still hard to
find him beneath the navy waves.

A tail of thorns lazes in the muddy depths feasting on
shellfish, sometimes a tasty mackerel if his steel jaws
move quickly. Those would be a more sustainable
menu choice, to enjoy on porcelain plates.

Cuckoo cloud dreams

Give me strength for this long passing so high

above the desert, endless flapping through the dark of night

then day then night then day then night then day and finally

give me a soft spring meadow warm for rest, where

pipit pipit tells me I am home, and give me a nest unattended

and the perfect moment to dart in and leave behind my own

delicately patterned to blend in, oh I know I will never
     see you

but again I must fly, high above the clouds over dusty Spain

4000 miles back to rainforest – please, give me strength.

Ode to a narrow-headed ant

Six-legged sun seeker;
Ingenious eco-builder.
Your 12-inch thatch absorbs the rays,
And retains warmth for cooler days.

You milk sweet aphids for survival;
Shield them in turn from foes and rivals.
Your formic cousins agitate:
Your response? Decapitate.

Notch-headed warrior, we pledge:
To conserve your glade and heathland edge.
You can't roam far to locate heaven,
Now make your final stand in Devon.

Your mighty Speyside stronghold
Undermined by threats untold.
Who'll spread rare small cow-wheat's seed,
Or give endangered capercaillies a feed?

'Protect the [   ]!' we entreat
As your habitat retreats,
And your future grows bleaker...
Six-legged sun seeker.

Pearl-bordered fritillary butterfly

Tickets on sale!
Book now: you don't
want to miss
my 2020 reunion tour.

Old stomping grounds
are closed, collapsed
replaced or reduced to
rubble. They resent
their ruin.

I was big in the seventies.
Soaring through spring flowers,
staying low and loose –
loving the life.

I lived large.

But the world changed.
Where does a pearl
bordered prince go?

You must have missed me,
sleeping in a leaf
wrapped at the bottom
of a stem.

I'm back.

Some say "[   ] is a sellout"
but my song needs to be sung.
Join my 2020 reunion tour:
tickets on sale.

When there's just 100 cod

Just 100 [   ] left
in the North Sea the headlines screamed
a fishy tale it emerged

perceptive perchance

[   ] the provider
bake fry poach
no fat just protein

and profit

no waste
what we don't eat sticks things
or makes our beer clear

nifty

profit spawned
hungry voracious predator taking more
until there are no more

in the sea

big [   ] make fecund fish
but deep draggers leave scanty spawners
ergo the small must grow big

to save the [   ]

and our 'fish and chips'
or 'fish' won't be [   ]
it will be whatever's left

when there's just 100 [   ].

The Haunting of the Harbour Porpoise

Bycatch of ghosts, bycatch by fishers.
A word that hides brutality
Death to our ocean introverts.

Barely disturbing the sea surface
They rise up, chuffing as they breathe
'Puffing pigs' their pet name.

An unwanted catch of fishers
Attending their nets, they rescue
Releasing [   ] from drowning.

Freedom to feed
Relentless, sleepless
Forever foraging.

Remembering journeys
Echoing songs
Searching for safe passage.

Ghost nets, unseen, unheard.
Floating spectres of abandonment,
Indestructible, a perpetual threat.

On their ruthless journey
Across undulating oceans.
Capturing, killing in their wake.

Save our shy, lonely friends
From becoming bycatch.
Bycatch of ghosts.

The Call of the Lesser Spotted Woodpecker

Before our decline (when we were only lesser in name, not lesser in nature) I remember flying, in our many thousands, undulating through tall tree tops on bright spring mornings. Flitting from branch to branch, our crimson crowns flashed brightly in the sunlight. And when the moon rose, we'd retreat to our hollowed-out homes in the trunks. Our song and our staccato peck are both, they say, unusually loud for such a small bird. Maybe that's because we urgently need to be heard, as they cut down our sanctuaries in the trees, and we remember a time before our decline.

Once A Jolly Koala Camped By A Billabong

Heed the warning: smoke is thick.

Along the roadside, charred and bloody remains of
a national symbol. The [   ] venture closer, crying,
screaming, begging for water. Habitat disappears
in a firestorm; those who survive are left homeless
and hungry.

Once a fluffy photo opportunity, jokes of "bears"
stoned on gumleaves. A third of the population now
gone, alongside **one *BILLION* other animals**.

This is not once-off. This is life now. The apocalypse
came; recovery is not guaranteed. A hotter, drier
climate makes the land a crackling tinderbox. All we
smell is pungent death.

Smoke is thick: heed the warning.

* A species native to Australia

A feminist therapist explains wild hamster decline

My dear child, Patriarchy Stress Disorder may have
any or all of the following symptoms:

An irrational belief in the scarcity of all things;
hoarding behaviour (BOGOF really means *Burrow of
Golden Oat Fortune*); stuffing one's face in a never-
ending cycle of self-care and home improvement

Being chased, caught, killed and sold for one's
skin so a spice merchant may line his coat with
a multicoloured, kaleidoscopic four-stanza
arrangement

Adopting dangerous-sounding bynames such as
'corn wolf', 'wolf of wall street', 'tiger of sales':
better to overpromise. No-one needs to know we're
the size of a guinea pig, my dear child.

* A species native to Eurasia, from Belgium to Russia

A Leap of Faith.

Would you please
listen.
If I tell you that I have no need for grand mansions
Or notions of self-importance.
No hankering for crowds nor limelight.
I am content with being still.
The epitome of mindfulness; c'est moi.
Some say I'm one out of the box.
That on the subject of family, I can trace mine back
    to the beginning of things
And from mine, I'll never stray; I have no interest
    in playing the field.
If I tell you that I'm not long for this world,
Would you overlook my insignificant stature,
And kiss me?
Would you,
please?

*A species native to New Zealand

Pangolin

An impossible animal uncoils,
Stretches from tip of scaly tail to scaly snout.
Stands on hind legs, sniffs the air.
Africa's artichoke totters into darkness.

Ants and termites scatter
As claws and snout tear into nest.
Tongue, sticky as a liquorice shoelace
Sucks up nature's pests.

For curious lion cubs
He curls up in a ball
Protected from claws and teeth
Beneath his armoured roof.

Against men this trick
Makes him easily portable property.

Boiled, burned or frozen,
Scales scraped from skin.
Meat or bad medicine.

But how long will we survive
When there's no longer
An impossible animal?

* A species native to Sub-Saharan Africa and Asia

Table for Two

"Sorry, madam, there's no [   ] left."

"But they're my favourite! I wanted them tonight to celebrate our anniversary. Are there really none left? Can you go and check, please?"

(Door swings into the kitchen)

"The lady on table 8 wants to know why there's no [   ]."

"That's the third table today, everyone wants them! Tell her they've been overfished – as far back as the Romans. That greedy lot loved [   ]. Then some American limpet stuck its oar in and shoved our [   ] out. I can't cook what doesn't exist!"

(Waiter approaches table 8)

"Sorry, madam, there's no [   ] left."

Heath fritillary butterfly

Fritter away not, flit-and-glide, survive, hide
Moon cycle, sun cycle, woodman's cycle
Egg_caterpillar_cocoon_butterfly
The world turns but never repeats.
Eat cow wheat, yellow under tasting feet,
speedwell, be well, lucky charm
Plunge proboscis in nectar sweet
Time will fleet.
Battle on the heath, military artillery,
a lined fence, first line of defence.
Decode orange intelligence,
a body in pieces, delicate feelers,
softly feel her, kneel before her
track and record her.
Open black arched back
fight dying light as sun sets
paper-thin velvet
Without [   ]
if all else remains, still strange
you forever forgot
Be with me always, fritter away not.

Empty Shelves

We know, now, what it's like to wake in spring
To empty shelves, and a quietening.

Think, then, of this long-tongued bumblebee:
                        shivering awake,
                                    crawling free,

just in time for the meadow's late-spring food–
–but there's no meadow, no bread for her brood.

                                        She sits,
                                        awaiting
                            a fragrant plume.

                The air is void.

It doesn't feel too soon for
                    knapweed

                                    woundwort

                    clover
                        vetch

yet not a single scent her senses fetch.

See that cropped field as she sees.
That arable desert was a flower-rich meadow

                        Swaying

                                    in a mid-June

                        breeze.

Where can she, the [   ], go?
Perhaps we know,

now.

Willow Tit, home bird

Home is life
Decline is rife

Black cap, twig legs, tiny beak
Out of the low shrub you peak
A [   ] meek, small
Until it's your turn to call

Zee Zee Zee, you sing
A distinctive, audacious ring
The [   ] private song
Only to you it could belong

But your song fades day by day
[   ] are you here to stay?
Many of your homes lost
At a devastating cost

Human need
Personal greed
No retreat
Your defeat

To survive
You need places to thrive
[   ] don't you shrink
Come back from the brink

Decline is rife
Home is life

Noble chafer

We hold on
Up in the cherry trees' cathedral heights.
I move the ladders for the women pickers,
Whose teasing makes me shy like the [   ].

As June tips into high summer, the true [   ] makes
   his entrance.
So long spent hiding, mere grub within his rotting
   bough.
Now a dandy in emerald silk jacket, stretching his
   wings in the sun,
Before shimmering off to meet his belle of the ball.

Today, housing estate stands tall, mighty orchard
   uprooted,
But the [   ]'s ancestral home was delicately
   transplanted
To the community orchard of young, squat trees
And together
We hold on.

Gone, before we knew it

And it disappears, sliding swiftly beneath the mossy log. Its slim body coiled tight, its round amber eyes peering out; assessing the risk.

And when it emerges, to weave through heather, its Harris Tweed coat proves cunning camouflage. So when the intent lizard sashays by, it barely sees the mouth that snatches it home.

Living undercover, the softly, softly snake, keeping its secrets close.

Yet we can still kill what we can't count or catalogue. With hate and housing and fire and farming, we've driven this creature from its heathland habitat. Just a few more human errors *and it disappears*.

Fen raft spider

Dr Helen Smith is Spiderwoman.
She hand-reared spider babies in her kitchen;
now thousands of them are thriving in the Fens
with superhero powers.
They walk on water; they turn silver when submerged.
Helen admires their mothering skills:
how the females build a careful cup of silk to lay
    their eggs in.
But even the most protective mother can't stop the
    climate changing.
I'd like to see them.
Instead I watch daddy longlegs scuttle beneath the
    rusting barbecue
while I Skype Mum on our balcony
and then, so she can spin a picture in my mind,
call Dr Helen Smith

Grey long-eared bat

pale-bellied long-lived slow-swooper
              you hear the dusty beat of moth
dry crick of lanky cranefly, sense the sudden glow
   of lacewing;
              Disney cartoon hyperbolic [   ] furry body
                 barely more
than the length of your huge ears, diaphanous as
   Tinkerbell's wings –
              curled back like horns under your
                 leathery cape
at rest in your cool [   ] cave.

                 We have pushed you to the margins
but still your warbling calls echo over monochrome
   nightmarsh
              inviting us to rewild;
let's plant yarrow, dill, angelica & caraway
              purple poppy mallow & marguerite –
                 come, feast on our feasting lacewings –
pale-bellied long-lived slow-swooper

Knot so common after all

Spring awakens them, parched and eager;
Polished amber globes like hornet headlights,
Nostrils pulsing like divining rods, dowsing to
find their target.

Toothless heads nuzzle through damp, rotted
leaves to emerge,
Primed and ready for the annual pilgrimage
To ancient birthing pools, where past and
future will meld.

A knot of urgency, justified in a world that mutates
During each winter sleep, breeding amorphous foes
Ignorant of lives lived in woodland walkways and
petri ponds.

Awaiting cover of dusk, naïve to its hidden hazards,
The not so common [   ]'s goal is
Rebirthing and renewal at all costs. Spring
awakens them.

Once more back home

Singing its name, called by Spring
[   ] starts from winter grounds
shaking dusty winds from its wings
compass set away to last Autumn.

Haven gives out to scrub, sand baked horizons,
foam blown water coloured by the sky,
air scented by greening landscape
zig zag human hazards and night time alerts.

Then land. Once more back home.

Home. Rich wilding hedges
flower spotted field edges,
or a peck through habitat destroyed,
no seed, bare nest, and one less song.

Fragile remnants of a storied past
echo through the winds of two continents
empty places, no longer singing its name.

You Cry Your Name

[   ] [   ] [   ]

under a mackerel sky –
gray scales flaked and flung
that speak of change

above the sea –
the wild wet prairie that you skim
mile after mile
while the wind scythes white spray
off the black-tipped waves

and you harvest the rising inches
of sandeels
slim, slippery strands to feed
the memory of wide raucous mouths
back on the narrow ledge
sparse horizontal
on the cliffs' stern vertical rise
and rise

and ask

this year? this year?

black-tipped wings
return mile after mile
and from that sweet face

you cry your name again, again
[   ] [   ] [   ]

Tiger Moth and Dolittle

'I have superpowers. I just need a name' said the girl.

'What are your powers?' I asked

'Well, obviously I can fly. I can use poison to
    fight baddies'.

'That's impressive, but why not call yourself what
    they usually call you?'

'What's that then?'

'[   ]'

'Ooh, cool name, I could live with that.'

She flew up and down and then landed beside me again.

'Hey' she said 'won't someone else have that name?'

'There's not so many of you these days, own it'.

'Okay. I never heard that name, I could never
    understand you big things. Why you?'

'I have superpowers'.

A Mountain Hare Mourns His Winter Coat

My disappearing act – March, hair by hair.

The North wind ruffles my winter-white pelage,
teasing out strands of my moult. They vanish, like
the trees, the Romans, the bears, the wolves, and
now [   ]

Landscape as mottled as I now am offers a choice
of snowhole or heather hollow. There to hide, nose
twitching, ears pricked, amber eyes wide.

Leveret no more, I can zigzag away when fox or
buzzard approach, though still I look up for the
eagle.

But here come men on chariots, with fire-sticks and
dogs, blaming us for their dearth of grouse.

My disappearing. Act!

Onna-bugeisha and the (White-Faced Darter)

She slips beneath the surface.
The warrior, who should be setting her stall.
An assassin of rare quality,
Primed to impale and consume disease-ridden enemies.
The [ ]
An Onna-bugeisha, jetting below the waterline.
She searches for her mossy sanctuary,
To lay down future armies in two-year slumber,
The nymph's creamy white face and jet-black eyes
Leaving no corner ignored.
And the earth waits,
Watching for the dancing spectrums of lacy wings
    to emerge
But they do not rise.
Sanctuary was not there.
The biters freed to feast instead.
And the [ ] does not return.
Silent waters,
After she slips beneath.

Fire and straw

Emerging from hibernation, the soft poppy-orange
tail of [   ] hope shivers
keeps close to the cool, mossy ground, bumbling
through the microclimate of a miniature caged
moorland understory
a pause
on a droplet-bowed petal
hardy enough to brave short days
and sharp winds
overlooked by grazers
hilltopping
then dancing down southern slopes
and buzzing along old pine wood carpets searching
out flowering blaeberry, bramble, and white clover
ambles from pink bell to purple bloom
black berry brimming
heather banks in the asphodel light of summer
    evenings
Chinese lantern pollen baskets
sipping sallow
this cold-lover emerging from hibernation.

Dear Glow-Worm

Dear [   ]

I write by the light
Of you and your comrades
While mine correspond
With sweethearts or mothers
I have neither
So address you
While we imperil
Humanity itself
In this shrieking mud-strewn hell

I trust we'll never
Imperil you
Sear the grasslands
That nourish snails
Which feed your larvae
(Which also glow!)
Confuse your efforts
To meet and mate
With our less efficient
Artificial forms of light

That my descendants
Are as dazzled as I, now
By the light from this jar
Trembling
But never faltering
As whizzbangs howl
And I pen the words

Dear [   ]

A rare sight

Visitors from afar, each [   ] unique.
Perfect brushstrokes across miniature canvas
Hidden amongst the long grass of fields
darting through dales and wooded groves,
of balmy summer evenings into the dwindling light
Juxtaposition of fragility and hardiness in one
    aerodynamic body
Conduit into nature, symbol of long-gone
    childhood memories,
British summertime and days gone by
Once found in swarms now a rare sight, embalmed
    on the pages of Castle Russell
Tiny beauty with paper-thin wings, will you remain
    in our skies?
An exotic gem, natural symmetry of caramel veins
    patterned across a perfect
wingspan
Chocolate brown migrants, visitors from afar.

ravens and writing desks

the table remains,
bare but for the cracked
teapot.
no mouse traps, no moon

no memory
nor muchness,
all vanished,
and the [   ] no longer sings in his sleep,
'twinkle twinkle little bat'.

mind you, that pool is new,
made from the tears that time
— not an it, but a HER —
wept for the waste,
for the abandoned
hedgerows and coppices.

'Wake up!' Alice cries,
but the hatter isn't here
to break the silence
and she still hasn't worked out

the elddir.

how can you take tea
when no one's left
to take it with you?

still, the table remains.

Pine marten: relocated

Can we start anew?

We trashed our home
Mother Earth waved
white flags
A solemn ceremony of
doleful surrender.

We let you go home
Slender pines waved
rugged arms
A sentinel's salute of
joyful remembrance.

Using wisdom from
machines
We s
   u
    b
     j
      u
       g
        a
         t
          e

Using wisdom from the
wild

You n   v   g   t
      a   i   a   e

Annihilate
Senses attuned to
Netflix
Gorging drive-thru
McFlurries
White men lynching
angrily
Within a
hyperconnected society
Devastating life for all
Natural animosity
Human skullduggery.

Reintegrate
Senses attuned over
millennia
Foraging tasty bilberries
Yellow bib flashing
playfully
Within a connected
system
Sustaining life for all
Natural reciprocity
[   ] recovery.

Can we start anew?

Scotland's Independent Feline Force: The Wildcat

Touch not this [   ]

Her stark refusal to be controlled, helped seal her fate.

Her intelligent, hidden face refusing to relinquish secrets, made enemies of those who wished to carve money from the land.

Kellas baudrons with his feral father and tendency to sicken, upon hearing of the death of the Queen of Cats, rushed up the chimney and claimed the crown of the Cat Sidhe.

But a blate cat maks a prood mouse

So mind, allow the Wullcat her throne, she means you no harm but will open up space in the land for all.

Touch not this [   ]

Water Vole as Billy Connolly

See me, Jimmy

I'm fae Glesgow,
by the M8.
that surprise you?

Nae wunner we moved,
came to whaur motors roared
sae close;
but nae humans, nae dugs
nae mink, only a kestrel shadow
overheid to keep an eye on,
an the stinkin' foxes.

Whit did we dae to youse
that you cut doon oor grasses,
blocked oor burns?

And they mingin mink,
they were yours too,
fur coats for ladies,
great idea that,
the buggers escaped
and gave us hell.

We spread from Spain,
We'll go further if we need to,
if you drive us further.

See me, Jimmy

Spotted flycatcher

Perching Egypt Bird
noted by Clare,
'Gray silent bird'
of Walter's poem,
the Bishop's
Beam Bird,
a 'Creature'
observed by Aitchison —
[   ] who will
write of you
in the future?
Of your
swiftly swooping,
deadly darting
flight?
Of your
way to de-sting
wasps?
Muscicapa striata
migrating to
and from Africa —
is that what
causes your
decline,
your high
mortality?

Or garden
predators watching
for absence
to plunder
your eggs?
[   ] even now
your 'tseep', 'eejip',
'squeaky wheel' song
is lost to many.
Gray-brown,
cream breast,
black legs,
the twitchers say,
but today [   ]
you are red
perching Egypt Bird.

Summer's Girl

A single egg
[   ]
reticulated pearl
prone on cock's foot, tor-grass, Yorkshire-fog
tucked in tussocks
dusted by dunes.
Gently uncapped by a caterpillar
who feeds to a chrysalis and
unravels to reveal an Edwardian lady.
She smooths her amber petticoats
takes flight
      skims crags, dances
         finds restoration on the balmy sand
            lingers to attract two black loving eyes
then lays the egg which
splits, feasts, cocoons.
But drawn early to wake
by the embers of an Indian summer
the child finds rocky outcrops barren
hemmed by spears of hollow straw
slows to a crawl
vanishes
[   ]
without
a single egg.

What right have we?

Feed, breed, burrow. The simple life of the [   ],
Europe's loudest amphibian. Thriving where other
amphibians can't, the [   ] has every spring for
millennia croaked out its mating chorus from pools
in salt marsh, lowland heath, and shifting sands.
Yet over the last century, 80% of UK populations
have disappeared. Moulding the landscape to
human ends, we've left the [   ] with few places to
call home. Is the [   ] important? Who knows. But
what right have we to drive its extinction? And if we
act now, restore habitats, create new ones, the [   ]
can still survive to feed, breed, burrow.

Stag beetle

When I fly,
You'll know it's late
As the sun starts to fade,
And life starts to slow.
Days left on earth after years spent below.

Time to go.
No rest for the wicked
As they say.

Coals that glow,
Cast into dusk.
The flare before the flicker.

Billywitch
Fiction, more fierce than the fact
Hornbug
Bark's worse than the bite
The fear was forged in the name;
The truth burns much less bright.

I wonder
Who will drum up the thunder
Who will carry the flame
Who will help the devil
Who will take the blame
When I fly.

Nightingale

His song soars to find her.
With bubbling grace notes
[   ] sends a sweet serenade through
the crystal stillness
of the night.

[   ] pauses, tilts his brown head
as if scanning his back catalogue.
With mournful tones,
the liquid voice fires
sorrow towards the stars,
lamenting losses
Of numbers
Of habitats.
Of futures.

Deep in the scrub,
an understudy joins in.
[   ] fluffs his lines,
losing the riff to the maestro.

Meanwhile, his song feels for the horizon
To eternal spring creeping north.

Towards the strongest singer,
she surfs the green wave to find him.

To [   ], his song soars.

Six things to do next

We hope that more people will take note and join our mission for nature's recovery, taking action for the wildlife that has given us so much.

1. Become a member of your local Wildlife Trust:
   www.wildlifetrusts.org/join

2. Experience wildlife in every season with family and friends:
   www.wildlifetrusts.org/visit/where-see-wildlife

3. Make sure your representatives know you care –
   find them here:
   www.theyworkforyou.com

4. Help wildlife at home:
   www.wildlifetrusts.org/actions

5. Ensure nature and people are integrated into local planning:
   www.gov.uk/find-local-council

6. Campaign for nature's recovery:
   www.wildlifetrusts.org/wilder-future

The Wildlife Trusts